Surround Your College Child with Prayer

Donna Jordan

Copyright © 2010 by Donna Jordan

Surround Your College Child with Prayer
by Donna Jordan

Printed in the United States of America

ISBN 9781609570040

www.xulonpress.com

Dedications

I dedicate this book to my son Jonathan (Jon), for whom I
pray, and pray, and pray. You, son, are a treasure.
I am so grateful that God sent you to me and allowed
me to be your mom. I love you.

I also dedicate this book to Dr. Ken Clapp, the "spiritual
authority" on Jon's college campus. Dr. Clapp, thank you
for your investment of prayer and godly influence
in Jon's life. It was very comforting knowing that you were
there during those four years.

Contents

Acknowledgements

I first thank my Lord and Savior Jesus Christ for calling, empowering, and enabling me to do this work. Thank You, God, for not giving up on me and this project.

I thank my wonderful husband for his faithful encouragement, support, and love. Lenny Hollabaugh, you are an incredible man and husband. Your unwavering support and encouragement cause me to believe that I really can do all to which God calls me. I love you forever, always, and 13 ½ days.

I thank Jonathan, my treasure of a son. Without you, son, there would be no book and much less prayer! ☺ You are a delight to my soul. I love you dearly.

I thank my dear friend Bonnie Murdoch for her willingness to draw the cover to match the image that God gave me (whether or not the publishers use it). What a beautiful job you did. I also thank you, Bonnie, for your prayers for Jonathan through these many years. Knowing that you care for him means so very much.

I thank Alice Cole-Snyder for partnering with me via email to pray our children's way through college. Alice, it was wonderful to connect with a mom who had a child in the same college as Jon. Thank you for your faithfulness to always be there and to cry out to God on Jon's behalf.

Dr. Clapp, you will never know how very much it blessed us to have you be a part of Jon's life on campus. Thank you that, even now, you continue to pray for him and invest in his life.

Thank you to my *Moms In Touch* prayer group. I joined these wonderful women after Jon was already in college. These incredibly faith-filled, praying women -- Meredith Barnes, Dina Breske, Roberta Edwards, Liz Evans, Donna Hoeflein, Lesa Lewter, Liz Mehailescu, Karen Ralston, Jessie Rollick, Beth Stanfield, and Laura Thaw -- enrich my life, encourage my faith, and enhance my prayers. Thank you, my wonderful friends, for "taking me in" and faithfully praying for my son. See you next week!

Introduction

I am so glad you picked up this book! To have done so, you must care greatly for your child and want the King of the Universe to intervene on your child's behalf. That is surely what I want for my son. I want God's desire and heart for Jonathan to be what his life reflects. It is my belief that the greatest thing I can do for him is to pray for him; and, I believe praying is the best thing that you can do for your child. That is why I have written this book.

College can be a scary time – for the parents of the college child! There are so many "what-ifs" when thinking of this new adventure in your young person's life. There is now what seems like a whole new world available to your child, one in which your part may seem small and obscure. You may have been accustomed, as I was, to knowing your child's friends and their families, to knowing what was going on and even where it was happening. Now, there may be times in which you merely think, "I don't have a clue..." and "I wonder..."

Even though you will not always know, you can entreat the One who knows it all. Entreat means to *make an earnest request of.* Only the Lord knows how earnestly I have made requests for Jonathan! As a parent who prayed mine and Jonathan's way through his four years of college, I want to assist you as you make requests of God for your college child. Because of my experiences, I wrote this book in a topical manner in order to give you specific areas of focus as you pray for your child.

The Scripture at the beginning of each chapter is related to that particular theme, but is certainly not exhaustive to that topic. I encourage you to read the Bible chapters from which each verse was taken. God's Word is so rich and deep, and by reading the verses in context you will gain a greater understanding of God's heart in relation to each topic. Also, I recommend that you search the Scriptures to find additional verses that relate to the topic for which you are praying. I believe this will greatly enhance your faith and trust in the One who gave us His Word.

The blanks in each prayer are there so that you can say your child's name or the words *him, her, he,* or *she* as you pray. I am hoping this simple format will enable you to be free to express yourself as you cry out for God's touch in your child's life. I pray that your prayers will extend far beyond my words. May you experience great peace as you surround your college child with prayer, knowing that God is the One who hears all.

1

Choice of College

James 1:5 "If any of you lacks wisdom, let him ask of God, who gives to all liberally and without reproach, and it will be given to him."

No matter where your young person is in the decision making process – just contemplating college, visiting them, or already enrolled – it is never too late to pray for wisdom that he or she will know the college that God has selected. God knows where He can best prepare your son or daughter for the future that He has in store. Along with this prayer for wisdom, pray for obedience for you and your child to follow through on what God reveals. As we prayed together as a family, we found it very helpful to listen to Jon's hopes for college and career. This enabled us to help him weed through the many college brochures that filled our mailbox. Once he had selected the three colleges that he was most interested in, we visited each of them. After leaving each campus, we made lists of the pros and cons associated with each.

Jonathan made the final decision based on where he believed God was leading, and we confirmed that decision. It was both interesting and surprising. He selected the one small college that was in a smaller town, and the campus was beautifully landscaped with trees and grass. He had clearly stated that he wanted to attend a big college in a big city – in a "concrete jungle" to be exact. My husband and I sincerely believed that Jonathan had chosen the college to which God had clearly directed. Yet, after his sophomore year, Jon visited two other colleges that he had researched and thought would better benefit him. After observing the shortcomings in these two schools, he became even more aware of how his school would best meet his educational needs, and so he remained. Pray about this choice as long as college or switching colleges is an option or a possibility for your child.

Father, You have promised to give wisdom to those who ask, and, Lord, I am asking for Your wisdom in our selection of a college for _____. I pray that _____ will seek Your wisdom as well. Lord, I believe that You know the best place for _____ to receive an education for the future that You have planned. You know from where the best preparation will come; Lord, reveal that to us, I pray. Let us hear You clearly, and let us be in one accord in this decision. Father, please give us the courage and conviction to obey Your direction. Thank You, Lord. In Jesus' precious name I pray, Amen.

2

Calm

Isaiah 26:3 "You will keep him in perfect peace, whose mind is stayed on You, because he trusts in You."

Without telling Jon that I was writing this book, I asked him what he would tell a parent who asked him for what he or she should pray for a child in college. He had just recently graduated and had experienced four years of an incredibly busy and intense program of study. If anyone could help me give you needed areas for prayer focus, I knew it would be him. He responded, "Calm, focus, and health." When I heard his answer I knew I had to pay attention, because this came from a young man who typically seems the epitome of calm. When I think of calm, I think of peace. I know from experience there is no peace like the peace that God gives. I have long considered Isaiah 26:3 to be my life's verse.

There is so much about college that could rattle your young person. From the mere thought of even going to college all the way through graduation, there may be many moments that are less than peaceful for your child. Wherever he or she is in the process, it is not too late to begin to pray calmness into his or her experience. The verse above says that God gives perfect peace to those whose mind is on Him. He becomes the focus in the many phases and decisions of life rather than any specific circumstance or situation. He promises to provide and "keep him" in this amazing peace irregardless of what is going on at any specific moment. His peace is not conditional upon circumstance. Pray that your young person is aware of this and makes God the focal point. As he or she does this, peace in the midst of all his or her circumstances will be the exciting and blessed reward.

Lord, the fact that we can experience any peace in the midst of a busy and hectic society is amazing. It is another testimony of Your incredible grace. Thank You, Lord. I pray that _____ will make You the focal point of life, so assuredly that _____ mind remains fixed on You. As _____ walks this college experience, may _____ be astounded at the peace You give in the midst of the many circumstances that _____ will face. Let _____'s heart and mind always be settled and at rest in You. May this peace be so evident in _____ life that others see You. I pray that _____ will be quick to give You the glory when others question the reason for such calm. Thank You, Lord. In Jesus' name, Amen.

3

Courage

Deuteronomy 31:6 "Be strong and of good courage, do not fear nor be afraid of them; for the LORD your God, He is the One who goes with you. He will not leave you nor forsake you."

First, pray courage into your own heart and mind so that you will be able to release your child to this new and exciting phase of life. Next, recognize that it takes courage for him or her to leave the familiar and step into the unfamiliarity of a college environment. I encourage you to commend your child for taking this positive, and possibly scary, step. Your son or daughter is displaying an admirable characteristic worthy of your recognition. Now that your child is entering into this phase, courage will be a consistent need if he or she is going to boldly embrace growth, pursue healthy experience, and stand firm on his or her convictions.

My pastor recently used this anonymous quote: "A coward dies a thousand deaths, but a man of courage only dies once." It is based on a similar quote by William Shakespeare. I do not know what Shakespeare had in mind when he coined his phrase, but in this phrase I think of the "coward" as someone who is fearful of what others think, so he panders to their decisions. He is afraid of doing things differently than everyone else, so he conforms to make sure that he does not stand out. He thinks he may not fit in, so he compromises his values. He fears rejection, so he follows because he is afraid to lead. I believe that each time a person such as this denies his or her own desires, values, and convictions, a part of that person dies on the inside. Each time is a painful experience. The pain gets greater as this person slowly becomes unrecognizable, even to self, and the once held dreams eventually die. Let's pray that courage continues to be a characteristic of your child.

Dear Lord, thank You for the courage You have placed within _____'s heart that enables _____ to step into this new territory. Thank You that You go with _____. I pray that You will make _____ever aware of Your presence and empower _____with courage to stand strong in who You have called _____ to be. May _____ walk courageously in everything to which You lead. May _____'s courage be a witness to Who You are, and may it encourage others to want this true courage and a relationship with the One who gives it. Lord, please bring like-minded friends into relationship with ___ __ so that they may encourage and strengthen one another. Thank You, Jesus. Amen.

4

Career

I Corinthians 12:18 "But now God has set the members, each one of them, in the body just as He pleased."

God has a career for your child. Because it is His choice, it carries great merit. You and/or your child may not feel that his or her choice of career or the strengths on which to build that career carry the same significance as other available choices. Perhaps the choice seems inadequate by comparison. After all, there are so many things your child could do with the future. God desires the whole body be fitted together for His purposes. So, yes, that means every position is valuable. More and more I understand the need for Christians to be actively engaged in every sector of society. If we are unwilling to take the light of Christ or to allow our children to carry that light into certain areas of society, there will be no light to dispel the darkness. Lives will go untouched and unchanged.

God began to reveal that truth to my very soul when my son shared with me his career desires. Jonathan was eleven when he told me that his interest was acting. Even though I inwardly cringed (I did not tell him about that☺), I smiled on the outside and proceeded to do what I could to encourage and provide opportunities for growth in that area. The Lord knew that the prospect of my son working in such an illicit and sinful area, as I saw the theater and film industry, was scary and disconcerting to me. A few years later, I remember telling Jonathan that God might use his incredible passion for acting to lead him to a different place, but one to which he would not have gotten except through his love of acting. By his second year of college his passion still included the theatre, but he had changed his focus to the technical aspect and he loved it! He now works as a technician with a touring theater group. Encourage your child's passions, and see where God leads.

Dear Lord, You are the giver of passion. You have said that You would fulfill the desires of our hearts. Thank You for the desires and passions that You have given to _____; even, God, if _____ is currently unaware of those passions. Reveal them, Lord, and help _____ to see the significance of the career choice to which You are leading. Help me, as _____'s parent, to see that as well. Strengthen _____ to follow your career guidance and direction. Please show _____ how this career will be used to glorify You in fitting together the body for Your purposes. I praise You for Your confirmation. In Jesus' name, Amen.

5

Salvation

Acts 2:21 "And it shall come to pass that whoever calls on the name of the LORD shall be saved."

I would be seriously remiss to presume that because you are holding this book your child is in a relationship with Jesus Christ. Perhaps you are not even actively involved with the One I've been writing about; the One to whom we have been praying for peace and guidance for your child. You might have picked up this book out of curiosity, or even desperation because your child is going away and you need to know that someone is watching over him or her. The verse above is for you as well. The gospel, the good news of Jesus and the salvation He offers, is available to all. John 1:12 fills my heart with such joy: "But as many as received Him, to them He gave the right to become children of God, to those who believe in His name." I encourage you to read John 3:15-17. Actually, I encourage you to read the entire book of John and discover, or rediscover, the incredible heart and love of Jesus. Romans 5:8 teaches that "God demonstrates His own love toward us, in that while we were still sinners, Christ died for us." You may already know personally this amazing truth and the awesome love of the Savior. If not, I hope you will today. If so, let's move onto your child.

I hope with you that he or she is in an active, intimate relationship with the Lord. But as we know, a saved parent does not genetically translate into a saved child. This is a decision that each person must make personally. The great news is that you can pray earnestly for the salvation of your child! Perhaps your child has accepted Christ as Lord and Savior at some point in his or her life, but is currently not walking in that relationship. Jesus did not move. He promised to never leave nor forsake His own. The Lord desires the return of fellowship with your son or daughter. Pray that your child will desire it as well.

Dear Lord, I praise and thank You that You have made salvation available to all who come to You. Father, I pray that _____ will desire relationship and fellowship with You through Your Son, Jesus, and by the power of Your Spirit. Lord, I pray that _____ accepts Your sacrifice, repents of sin, and seeks Your forgiveness. I pray that _____ will love and serve You. If _____ has accepted You previously but the relationship has grown lukewarm or cold, restore _____ to Yourself, Lord. Let _____ fall before You and seek rededicated fellowship with You. May _____ choose to walk in intimate relationship with You always. Thank You, Jesus. Amen.

6

The Armor

Ephesians 6:11 "Put on the whole armor of God, that you may be able to stand against the wiles of the devil."

If there is any place that the strategies and plans (the wiles) of the devil are going to attempt seduction of your child, it is college! I remember visiting Jon on Halloween weekend during his freshman year. I soon realized that being on the campus at 11:30 p.m. was not a good idea. The later it got, the stranger some young people seemed to think they had to act and dress. I was stunned to see such lewdness and perversion from people so young. My heart was grieved that they were so lost. By lost, I am not necessarily referring to salvation. I sensed they were losing themselves in deception of what was truly fun and freeing. Let me just say that I went home with a much longer prayer list. In fact, every time that I visited the campus for the first couple of years, I came away knowing that God had allowed me to see much so that I would pray much. In all honesty, it was often agonizing. In spite of the pain and concern, I became thankful that God was revealing to me how I should pray.

He is so gracious to give us revelation and understanding. I have often prayed to "put on" His armor. However, God revealed to me recently that the armor is much more than something to be prayed "on" – it is something to walk in consistently. This is done by walking faithfully and consistently in Christ. The Word says to "take up the whole armor" (v. 13). If we are actively walking in His righteousness, in the truth of His Word – in all the attributes mentioned in association with the armor pieces – then we are wearing the armor as we walk this life. Let us pray that your child walks a faithful life in Christ, and, thus, will be protected by His armor.

Father, I desire that _____ be protected from the wiles of the enemy. My prayer is that _____ will stand against these schemes rather than fall victim to them. God, Your Word says that as _____ puts on Your whole armor, _____ will be able to stand and not fall. Oh, Lord, strengthen and empower _____ to walk a faithful and consistent Christian life in Your Spirit, protected by Your armor. Cause _____ to walk in truth, righteousness, peace, faith, salvation, and Your Word. Give _____ a desire to stay close to You, I pray. Thank You, Mighty God. In Jesus' name, Amen.

7

Dorm

1 Corinthians 15:33 "Do not be deceived: 'Evil company corrupts good habits.'"

Have you ever heard comments such as "the party dorm," "the cool dorm," or "the druggie dorm"? Ask students on just about any college campus to tell you about the dorms and you will likely hear such descriptions. It can make a parent want to set his or her child up in a private apartment! The reality of college life is that it is already going to take a strong proactive mindset for your child to avoid the corruption of "evil company" on the campus and in classes. Pray that he or she is in a dorm, and at the very least on a hall, where there is a break from such companionship. The living atmosphere surrounding your college child has the potential to be very influential in his or her life. A young college friend recently told me that she lived on a hall that was mostly filled with Christians, and this was at a non-Christian college. She would often go down the hall and hear worship music coming from various rooms. It was a great comfort to her that so many like-minded people lived on her hall. She and several of her hall mates held weekly Bible Studies.

College dormitory selection is sometimes determined simply by what year of college the student is entering. Often there are specific dorms that are only for freshmen, upperclassmen, etc. That supposed certainty could dissuade you from praying for the best dorm or hall selection for your child, believing that there are no choices. This may seem to be the case for your child, but remember that God makes a way where there seems to be no way. God has just the right living arrangement in which your college child can thrive. Ask for it!

Oh Lord, You know my heart and desire for _____ to live in a clean and wholesome environment. Father, I pray that _____ will be in a place surrounded by people who will influence _____ for good, not evil. Lord, please intervene in the dorm selection and put _____ right where You want _____ _ to live. Only You know the very best dormitory for _____. Put _____ in a dorm or hall in which there is a thriving and positive atmosphere, not one of corruption and evil. Protect _____ from evil company and let _____ live in a place of life and growth, not death and decay. Thank You, Lord, for Your selection and protection. In You I trust. Amen.

8

Roommate

Philippians 2:2 "Fulfill my joy by being like-minded, having the same love, being of one accord, of one mind."

My husband and I thought we had prayed about everything in the most specific ways imaginable when Jon was entering college. Yet, two weeks into his freshmen year he switched dorms and roommates, and told us after the fact. A young man in their freshmen dorm was being picked on and provoked. Jon, with his considerate and compassionate heart, agreed to room with this young man so the guy would not have to pay a single room rate for not having a roommate. Oh my, did we ever quickly discover the need to pray for so much more than we had thought and even more specifically! This young man had serious emotional issues which were manifested by perversion and extreme sloppiness. As a result, Jon spent most of his time that year everywhere but in his room. Our hearts ached that he could not make himself comfortable and really settle in during his first year.

His last three years on campus were spent in a small dorm designated for sophomores, juniors, and seniors who maintained a certain grade point average. His roommate for two of those years was a godly young man who was not ashamed of the love he had for his Lord and his country. This young man chose his friends wisely and entertained guests quietly and respectfully. His care and thoughtfulness to Jon and Jon's feelings was very evident. They were like-minded in their love for the Lord and their consideration for each other, although I think they rarely spoke of either. Prior to Jon's senior year, we were told that his roommate for that year was to be a young man living the homosexual lifestyle. Instead, in answer to prayer, Jon roomed alone his last year of college. God can create miracles in any situation. Don't be afraid to pray for them.

Father, I cry out to You for _____'s roommate. Lord, I ask for someone who will be like-minded with my child. Let them be of one accord and one mind when it comes to the details of the room and the decisions regarding guests and entertainment. Lord, I pray that they will respect one another and truly care for one another as friends. Build a strong, lasting friendship between _____ and _____ roommate. I pray salvation, protection, and wisdom for _____'s roommate. May they encourage and sharpen one another as each walks with You. Let them work together well, resolve disagreements quickly, and learn from one another. May their relationship be healthy and pleasing in Your sight. Thank You, Lord Jesus. Amen.

9

Professors

Psalm 43:3 "Oh, send out Your light and Your truth! Let them lead me…"

Referring to the scripture above, the footnotes in my Bible read: *"Only the 'true light' of God could save the psalmist from the lies and darkness all about him."* This reminds me of an incident that Jon experienced with one of his professors. The day after a national election, this particular professor came into class wearing all black (she might even have worn a veil, I don't quite remember), was in a somber mood, and just sat at her desk with her head hung down as if she was in great grief. That was the atmosphere in which the students spent their entire class period. Instead of doing her job and instructing the students regarding their subject material, she conveyed her disappointment that the liberal candidate she had supported was not elected. Although Jonathan was one of perhaps two students who had not supported her candidate, and, thus, did not take on the oppressive mood, it bothered me that his class time was spent that way and that our tuition was paying for such manipulation and incompetence.

Professors have an enormous impact on impressionable, young minds and they know it. They hold positions of power over young people who have little power and no position. Not only can this power intimidate our children, but some professors are also such know-it-alls that students feel pressure to conform to the professors' opinions. Let's face it, educators can influence for good or evil. It is most unfortunate that evil seems to be prevailing through the teaching of secularism and humanism. It does not have to remain that way. I believe that God has people in every sector of society who reflect His light and truth. There are professors who use their influence for good, and we will pray for them to be a part of your college child's life.

Oh Lord, it grieves my heart to think of anyone attempting to influence my child with darkness. Father, I rebuke every attempt of the enemy to use professors to wrongly influence _____, in the name of Jesus. I pray that _____ will have professors who speak truth in every subject. May each class be a class of revelation and knowledge on which _____ can build the life You have in store for _____. I pray that You stop the mouths of those who insist on teaching against Your principles and ways. Lord, I pray for godly professors who will bring Your light and Your truth to bear, and who will in no way pervert the education You have ordained for _____. Thank You for Your protection and provision in this area. Amen.

10

Purity

2 Timothy 2:22 "Flee also youthful lusts; but pursue righteousness, faith, love, peace with those who call on the Lord out of a pure heart."

Suddenly, it is as if the world is poised to give your child plenty of opportunity to express his or her individuality, the unsupervised time to examine new interests, and the freedom to explore and experience adventure. Your young person is probably feeling ready for it! After all, he or she has possibly felt that the world was small and restraining up to this point. Now is the time for an exciting new outlook. There is such an enthusiasm for life that comes with youth. That, of course, is a wonderful thing. If one is not careful, though, some enthusiasm can become so intense as to develop into lust. College provides an atmosphere that could carry your young person along on a sea of creating lusts and then fulfilling them. Notice the word, "carry." No activity is required for the one being carried or caught in the drift.

To *flee*, however, is a very different story. Fleeing is certainly an active choice. One is usually not seen running unless he or she chose to run. The choice was purposeful;

it was not made by default. It seems that youthful lusts are a given, a natural part of life. So in order to flee these lusts, one must make the decision and then make a move. Now read the scripture again. To flee is not going to be enough for your child, although it is a great move. He or she then needs to be active (again) in order to pursue the things that are going to promote and fulfill healthy, life-giving enthusiasm. These types of enthusiasm will bring enrichment, fruitfulness, purity, and abundant life. Let's pray that your young person actively chooses not to be a drifter.

Lord, there is so much in the world today that could suck my child right into a life of lust and loss. I pray, Father, that _____ will hear Your voice saying, "Flee!" Empower _____ to obey and let _____ choose that obedience every time. If _ _____ should fall, Lord, please quickly set _____ feet back on the right path. May _____ not drift through life, but instead be proactive to make good choices. I pray for strength and courage to rise within _____'s heart. Let _____ be quick to pursue the things of the Lord. Give _____ a desire for the things of You, Lord, which is greater than any other craving. Protect _____ and keep _____ alert, I pray. In Jesus' name, Amen.

11

Campus Life

1 Corinthians 10:13 "No temptation has overtaken you except such as is common to man; but God is faithful, who will not allow you to be tempted beyond what you are able, but with the temptation will also make the way of escape, that you may be able to bear it."

If I learned one thing more than any other during Jon's college years, it is that there is always plenty of action on college campuses – and much of it takes place after midnight! It could simply include getting together to watch a movie, attending a college-sponsored event, or partying. Your child will have many activities from which to choose. There is a broad range of events going on nearly all the time. Temptation is an issue your child may face, and face often. These temptations will not always necessarily involve what we may think of as sinful things, although I think there will be plenty of those. It could be something as simple as your child being tempted to not do his or her assignments because of boredom or tiredness. Maybe skipping classes seems like a good idea because no one is there saying, "You have to go." These are not temptations that would necessarily lead to sin, but they could certainly have an adverse affect on grades.

As the verse says, God will make a way for your young person to escape from the snare associated with temptation. I can remember times that my husband and I visited Jon and he would mention that certain events were taking place on campus. I often whispered, "Thank You, Lord, that we are here this weekend so he did not have to seriously consider whether or not he would attend." I believe, in those instances, we were God's provision of escape. Also, Jon's program of study was the most involved on campus and required so very much hands-on time that he "escaped" much action. I was sometimes displeased that he was so bogged down with work that he could not participate in other worthy activities. I was thrilled, however, when it kept him from potentially harmful or sinful situations. Whatever the temptations your child may face on campus, pray that he or she finds and chooses the way of escape.

Thank You, Dear Lord, that You promise to provide a way of escape each time _____ faces temptation. Please give _____ wisdom to see the way and the confidence to walk in it. Help _____, Lord, to make good choices when determining what to do on campus. Put obstacles in _____ path, if necessary, to keep _____ from falling to temptation. Give _____ courage and strength to resist pressure and to choose what is pleasing in Your sight. Surround _____ with strong, positive influences who will make it easier for _____ to make good choices. Let _____'s time on campus be filled with wholesomeness and growth. Thank You, Lord. In Jesus' name, Amen.

Influence

Romans 12:2 "And do not be conformed to this world, but be transformed by the renewing of your mind..."

As a parent, I have given much thought to the fact that every person with whom Jon comes in contact has the potential to influence him in some way. That is why, for several years now, I have prayed for every person he has mentioned by name. I want to affect their influence in Jonathan's life through prayer and the power of the Holy Spirit's intervention. I add each name to a list so that I will remember to pray for them. Even long after he ceases to mention them, I continue to pray for their salvation, walk with the Lord, and their lives. I also pray for God to pave Jon's way with committed and fun-loving Christians who will influence him with their steadfast devotion to Christ. I cry out to Him to fill the theatre and entertainment industry with people who will shed His light into this dark sector of society.

I am not afraid to implore God to remove someone from Jon's life if I feel that their influence is harmful to him and his walk with the Lord. I have prayed that way many times. I also pray about the influence that Jon will have on others. If I ever felt that he was behaving in a manner that could hurt

someone, I then prayed for their protection from his influence, and his removal from their lives if necessary. I want
him to be transformed, as God does it – from the inside out
– not conformed to the ways of man and the world. Your
young person will most likely meet many, many people in
college. Some of these people will hold ideas that seem foreign, and your child may experience pressure to conform to
others' ways of thinking. Pray that your child's formation
comes from the renewing of the mind, not the influences on
campus.

Lord, Your Word commands that transformation come
by the renewal of the mind. Please renew _____'s mind and
transform _____ from the inside out. Let _____ choose not
to conform to the ways of those around _____ whose influence could bring harm. Father, bring people into _____'s
life whose influence is for good. Remove from _____'s life
those who will influence in opposition to Your will. I pray
for _____'s protection from harmful and hurtful influences.
Cause _____ to be one of those whose influence is for You
and Your kingdom. Let my child be a positive influence on
those with whom contact is made. I pray for those around
_____ to know, love, and serve You. May You be the greatest
influence in _____'s life. Thank You, Lord. Amen.

13

Direction

Psalm 119:133 "Direct my steps by Your word, and let no iniquity have dominion over me."

This verse is a prayer all by itself. I have prayed it regularly, inserting Jonathan's name, since March 3rd, 2004. That was the day the Lord showed it to me and revealed its' importance as a prayer. I wrote it down that day on an index card and placed it on the counter of my bathroom. It only gets removed for cleaning, and afterwards it goes right back so that my husband and I have a visual reminder to pray this powerful prayer. Imagine for yourself the power of the very Word of God directing your children's steps, their direction in everyday moments as well as life-altering decisions. I believe this Word is written (the Bible), and it is the voice of the Lord (the Holy Spirit) speaking directly to our children's hearts saying, "...This is the way, walk in it..." (Isaiah 30:21).

The word *dominion* denotes control and sovereignty. The fact that *iniquity* and dominion are even used in the same sentence should be enough to awaken a parent's prayer life. From your own experiences, you may realize the incredible power the lure of sin and iniquity hold. To think that anything outside of God's sovereignty could direct and control a child—your child, my child—is alarming. However, because they are human beings and were born into a sinful, fallen world, they are susceptible to all the frailties that come with humanity. That is the bad news. Now for the good news. Jesus' death and resurrection, through the power of the Holy Spirit, provides the way for them to overcome the sin and depravity of their humanity. God's Word can protect them and prevent them from falling prey and becoming subject to any power other than His own. Let's pray His Word over your child now!

Father, in the powerful name of Jesus, I ask You to direct _____'s steps by Your Word, and let no iniquity have dominion over _____. I pray that _____ will know and heed Your Word, and that Your Word will become a shield and a refuge for _____. Lord, keep _____ from iniquity. If _____ is engaged in any sin that could become a stronghold for _____, Father, please rescue _____ now, I pray. Bring Your truth and light to bear on this iniquity and reveal to _____ what steps _____ is to take to be freed. Let not anything or anyone control _____ but You, my Lord. Teach _____ by Your Word and Spirit, and let _____ direction come solely from You. Thank You, God, for Your mighty Word. Amen.

14

Uncompromising Excellence

Daniel 6:3 "Then this Daniel distinguished himself above the governors and satraps, because an excellent spirit was in him; and the king gave thought to setting him over the whole realm."

Whenever I hear the word *compromise*, I think of Daniel and how he did not compromise his beliefs when he was taken completely out of his comfort zone to a foreign land. From much of what I witnessed on visits to Jon's campus, college might just be considered a foreign land! I have often wished that Jon's dad and I had included the name Daniel somewhere in Jonathan's name. Maybe he could have been Jonathan Lee Daniel Jordan. I recently told Jon that I was adding Daniel to his name, if only in my mind. He, of course, thought I was becoming a bit weird, or perhaps weirder. I like Daniel's legacy, and I desire that "excellent spirit" and uncompromising nature for my son. So, if adding Daniel to Jon's name helps me to remember to pray that he will be a man of integrity, excellence, and one who will not compromise the things of God, then J.L.D.J. it is.

Compromise is a slippery slope. Once the slipping begins, headlong destruction is on the way. Just as we do not always know that the ground beneath our feet may be slippery, we may not always be aware that we are compromising. Sometimes we are just too busy or too noisy to hear the voice of the Holy Spirit as He attempts to warn us that we are heading down that slope. Many times it is a subtle thing and catches us off guard, just as ice beneath our feet causes us to suddenly and surprisingly slip. We know it can be a battle to stand on solid ground and maintain our footing. That knowledge is why it is so important for us to pray that our children will be wise and uncompromising. We must surround them with prayers for wisdom, strength, and an excellent spirit. Your college child will most likely be inundated with opportunities which could lead to compromising his or her values. Let's pray that your young person maintains sure footing.

Dear Lord, I pray that You give to _____ sound wisdom so that _____ is able to discern compromising situations. Direct _____'s path so that _____ avoids the slipping away from You that compromise causes. Help _____ to stand strong and on the sure ground that a relationship with You affords. Lord, I ask that You clearly signal the wrong way with many red flags and that _____ will heed those warnings. Strengthen _____ to make the right decisions, and give _____ courage to not falter. Place within _____ an excellent spirit, I pray. Give _____ like-minded friends to walk with _____ and to hold _____ up to You. Thank You, Dear Lord. Amen.

15

Hope

Romans 15:13 "Now may the God of hope fill you with all joy and peace in believing, that you may abound in hope by the power of the Holy Spirit."

Hope is both a noun and a verb. As a noun, the Webster's 1828 Dictionary describes it as, "That which gives hope; he or that which furnishes ground of expectation, or promises desired good." God is hope. He definitely furnishes us with a firm ground of expectation in Him, and His promises are for our good. He is also the giver of hope. As a verb, Webster defines hope: "To place confidence in; to trust in with the confident expectation of good. To cherish a desire of good, with some expectation of obtaining it, or a belief that it is obtainable." After reading those definitions, it finally made sense to me why some people say that hoping in the Lord is expressing confidence just as if they had prayed.

I have already discussed your child's salvation, so I am hoping with you that he or she has made Christ the Hope of life. I now want to agree with you that your child will be filled with hope; that your son or daughter will expectantly and confidently seek the things that the Lord has placed in his or her heart. It is too easy to get caught up in wishing for things to happen. Although many of us use the words wish and hope interchangeably, they are not the same. To wish, according to Webster, implies a longing for something that is likely not obtainable and is often accompanied by anxiety. Worry and fretting often accompany wishing, whereas a confident expectation accompanies hope. Let us pray that your college child's hope is found in the Lord, and that he or she pursues hope, not wishes.

Oh Lord, You are so many "things" to us! Thank You for being the very Hope on which we can have a solid ground of expectation. Thank You, Lord, that You have provided a way for us to know You, and to have confidence in and through You. I pray that You, the God of Hope, will fill _____ with all joy and peace in believing, and that _____ may abound in hope by the power of Your Holy Spirit. The world does not inspire hope, but You do. Reveal to _____ the differences in hoping and wishing, and let _____ cling to the hope You provide. Let _____ confidently hope and believe for all that You have placed in _____ heart. May _____ obtain, with hope, all that You have in store for _____ life. In Jesus' name, thank You, and Amen.

16

Protection

Psalm 91:4 "He shall cover you with His feathers, and under His wings you shall take refuge; His truth shall be your shield and buckler."

As I write this chapter, it is just days past the "Miracle on the Hudson." A commercial airliner landed on the Hudson River and all occupants exited safely. A miracle indeed! Praise His holy name! To think of such protection and provision from the hand of Almighty God excites me, and it comforts me as well. This story illustrates that I can trust my child to God, knowing that He cares even more for Jonathan than I do. The love and concern I have for him is immeasurable; and when I remember that the God who holds jets in His hands also holds Jon, I know I can rest in His protection of Jonathan's mind, body, and spirit.

I want to encourage you, as well, to trust God for the protection of your child. Your child is not jetting around the college campus in an airliner, but you know there are reasons for concern. There are dangers and pitfalls lurking from a real enemy who wants to bring down your son or daughter. Threats of intense secularism abound on many campuses. There is most likely pressure for your young person to conform to the environment, rather than transform it. There are safety issues surrounding his or her new-found freedom to be out and about all hours of the night. There is the unknown and the unfamiliar for your child, but also for you because you are not there to be aware of everything. Of course, let us not forget there is the stuff that you do know about which sends you quickly to your knees! Only God can shield and protect your child in these, and all circumstances. Pray for His protection.

Almighty God, I praise You that You alone are all-powerful and all-knowing. You know what is in my child's future. Moment by moment You are fully aware. I thank You for that, and Lord, I thank You that You care. Father, I ask for Your divine protection over _____. Lord, hold _____ in the palm of Your hand and shield _____ from danger and all harm. Protect _____'s mind, body, and spirit from all that is not of You. Let not the enemy prevail in any area of _____'s life. May _____ walk in great wisdom, discernment, insight, and strength, which all come from You. Lord, teach _____ to guard _____ heart and mind with all diligence. May _____ walk safely and securely all the days of _____ life because of Your protection over _____. Thank You, my Dear Father, for protecting my child. Amen.

17

Confidence

Proverbs 3:26 "For the Lord will be your confidence, and will keep your foot from being caught."

How many times has a lack of confidence caused you to feel caught or trapped? You found yourself bound and nearly paralyzed by a fear that you did not measure up, or you weren't good enough, or you were simply incapable. There are too many "I am less than" thoughts to mention. I have been there way too often. I did not step out to take action during those times. I avoided people, places, and things; and, as a result, I accomplished little. What a hindrance it was to be caught up in that. It prevented me, for so long, from moving towards being all God called me to be, and it kept me from doing many things He had called me to do. Whew, those were exhausting periods in my life. It takes great energy to fight against who God says we are; just as it is depleting to listen to what the world says about us.

Imagine the struggle your young person could have regarding this issue. He or she does not have the advantage of your personal experience and wisdom which has taught you that personal identity is not found in what the world thinks. Many young people today are less than confident about themselves. Your child does not have to be one of them. He or she is God's workmanship created in Christ Jesus (Ephesians 2:10); a design of the King. Jonathan knew this, and he was a pretty confident young man when he left home for college. In college I saw this confidence wane somewhat, and he was affected in ways he had not previously experienced; at least, not openly. I watched him struggle in some areas in which he had once been fairly secure. It was tough to watch. Because of my experience, I know that the potential for your child to struggle is real. Let's support him or her in prayer.

Lord, You will be _____'s confidence if _____ will let You. I pray, God, that _____ will. I pray that _____ finds _____ confidence in You and what You have to say about _____ ___. Deafen _____'s ears to lies and confusion, and deaden the affects of what the world may say about _____. _____ is who You say, and that is all that matters. Make this a reality in _____ life. I pray that _____ will walk an active, close walk with You which will enable _____ to be strong and confident all of _____ days. Thank You, Lord, that _____ can find confidence in You and not self. Thank You that we do not have to try and manufacture it, for we know that would not last. In You, we are secure. Thank You, Jesus. Amen.

18

Study

2 Timothy 2:15 "Be diligent to present yourself approved to God, a worker who does not need to be ashamed, rightly dividing the word of truth."

Even though I now primarily use the New King James Version, I often remember verses according to the King James Version (KJV) because that is how I learned them in my younger days. In the KJV, the above verse begins with the word, "Study." I like to put them together and say, "Study diligently." My desire is that your child and mine will diligently study the Word of God and grow in the knowledge of Him. I believe this is from where true wisdom comes and direction is given. Reading the Word of the Lord establishes and nurtures relationship with Him. Knowing Him and about Him will inspire and enhance interactive communication among our children and Him. This type of study is the most productive, and I believe it creates a foundation on which God can then use other study in our children's lives.

Someone, whether it is you, your child, family, friends, companies, the college, or the government, is paying a high financial price for your son or daughter to attend college. You most likely want your child to make the most of this opportunity, and to learn the material so as to benefit for the future. There will be many on-campus opportunities for your young person to do something other than study and prepare for class. Jon sometimes took advantage of other opportunities, and occasionally his work suffered. Thankfully, he had begun college (and continued) with the determination that he wanted to learn so he would be prepared for the future when he graduated after four years. He was quite surprised when he discovered that many students turned a four-year degree program into five years. There were some understandable causes, of course, but the majority seemed to just not want to put the necessary time and effort into studying. Let us pray that studying will be an important part of your child's education.

Dear Lord, more than anything I want _____ to know You. Please reveal to _____ the importance of studying Your Word and give _____ a desire to do so. And, Father, as _____ takes college classes, I ask that You give _____ a desire and determination to study and learn all that will benefit and prepare _____ for the future. Help _____ to focus on the important activities and not to become distracted by the many people and activities available on campus. I pray that _____ will have a healthy balance of engaging in fellowship, friendship, and study. Give _____ wisdom and obedience to know how to use _____ time wisely, I pray. As _____ studies, open _____ mind to understand and comprehend all that is needed. Give _____ insight, discernment, knowledge, retention, and articulation, I pray. In Jesus' name, thank You, and Amen.

19

Being

Acts 17:28 "For in Him we live and move and have our being..."

It is difficult to just *be* in society today. We must *do*. People are often measured and summed up by what we do. We are performance driven, or so it seems. Listen to conversations around you as people are introduced to one another. One of the first questions asked is, "What do you do?" When is the last time you heard someone say, "Who are you? Tell me about yourself."? It was just a few years ago that I was first introduced to the concept of a *human doing*. (I then realized that I had lived as one for many years.) That is not what we are, we are human *beings*. Unfortunately, many of us have forgotten how to be: to be who God created us to be; to be in His presence; to be content with who we are; to be a precious child of the King.

It would be too easy for your child to find his or her identity in actions and accomplishments. As it is, there will be lots to do at college in order for your child to gain knowledge and graduate. Those things will be necessary, but they will not say who your child is. Yes, we must do in life to get things done. We can not just sit around being. It is really all about the focus. In doing, the focus is on self and what self can do. In being, the focus is on God and what He can do through us. It is then that our attention is directed in the right place. It is my belief that it is crucial to your child's sense of well-being for him or her to recognize that a healthy sense of self is found in the One in which we have our being. Let's pray for God's truth to define your child.

Father, it is so easy to get caught up in the many things that need doing, and before long life becomes about what needs to be done. Lord, I pray that my child's life will be complete in You, and that _____ will be faithful to the tasks/ work that You have for _____ to do. Lord, protect _____ from confusing personal identity with performance. Remind _____ that in You we have our being. Give _____ a healthy sense of self that tells _____ who _____ is in You. Do not let _____ take on the lies of the world and the enemy as they attempt to define _____ by _____ actions and accomplishments. May _____ discover fully who You are and who You say _____ is. Thank You, Lord, for Your affirmation over my child. Amen.

20

Spiritual Authority

Titus 2:15 "Speak these things, exhort, and rebuke with all authority. Let no one despise you."

I use the term "spiritual authority" to describe Dr. Clapp's position on Jon's college campus. He is actually the Vice President and the Chaplain. One of the first things that my husband and I did when Jon began college was to introduce ourselves to Dr. Clapp and give him Jonathan's name. We asked him to pray personally for Jon by name, and to, also, when possible, draw Jon into the campus activities that were about the Lord. We kept in touch by email sharing prayer requests; us for Jon, and he for campus, faculty, and student concerns. We would stop by his office to talk when we visited Jonathan. He connected me with another Christian college mom so that we could pray together via email. He is a man of integrity and faithfulness who cares deeply for the students he serves. We were very comforted and encouraged knowing that he cared so much for the students, and that he was personally reaching out to Jonathan and praying for him.

Even though Jon's college was secular, I believe that God gave Dr. Clapp, through his position of Chaplain (and personal relationship with Christ, first and foremost), spiritual authority to influence the students for Him. Your child's campus may not have a designated Chaplain or Pastor, but chances are great that someone working there knows Christ personally and is praying for the students. Listen to your child as he or she talks about the faculty. The Lord can reveal to you who He has at work on the campus. My encouragement to you is that you try to get to know them and have them know your son or daughter. Encourage this positive influence in your child's life. Whether you meet these people or not, pray that God strengthens and sustains those on campus who are striving to make a difference for Him. Pray that God brings others to stand with them. Encourage these authorities when you have the opportunity, and, above all, pray for them.

Gracious Lord, I pray that You raise up spiritual authorities on my child's college campus. Let them be people of integrity and godliness. Lord, I pray that _____ will be in their path and will be influenced by them for good. Build healthy, godly relationships between them and my child. Dear Lord, I pray for these people to be strengthened and encouraged. Father, I ask for Your protection over them and pray that You keep them from becoming weary. I pray that You will raise up many others so they can stand together for truth and Your values. Lord, I pray for revival to sweep across my child's campus, and let my child be a part of it. Thank You, Lord, that You have people at work for Your kingdom on _____'s campus. Amen.

21

Parents

Colossians 3:21 "Fathers, do not provoke your children, lest they become discouraged."

Wait a minute, this book is supposed to be about the children, not the parents! You, as a parent, are an instrumental part of your child's life. It is important to cover yourself in prayer in relationship to your child. For you to be aware of what is going on in your son or daughter's mind and life, sometimes it is only the wisdom of the Lord that is going to provide the information. While growing up, Jonathan many times said to me, "You are smart!" As he got older, he realized, of course, that it was not really me but the Holy Spirit who was so smart. There were still those times, though, that he seemed in awe that I could comment or ask a question that spoke right to what he was pondering. Many valuable conversations ensued as a result. These times were only able to happen because I had prayed that God would give me insight and discernment into Jon's heart.

Now that your child is college-aged and becoming an adult, your job, I believe, is to not so much parent as to mentor, coach, and befriend. Your parenting, or rearing, days are over. Now, hopefully, you get to reap good fruit from your years of labor. I have discovered that trying to parent a young adult is often a quick way to both provoke and discourage. This does not mean that you now have nothing to add to your child's life, nor does it mean that he or she knows it all. What it means is that you adjust the words and the way in which you share guidance and direction. This may look different for you than it did for me, and it may look different with each child. The important thing is to seek God's heart for your child and to act accordingly.

Father, I thank You for the privilege of having raised _____ _; a precious treasure sent right from You. Lord, please show me how to encourage and help _____ without parenting. Help me to coach, mentor, and befriend _____ in a way that pleases You and brings glory to Your name. Lord, I pray that You will give me discernment and insight into _____'s heart and mind. Help me to speak the words and ask the questions that will cause _____ to open up and share with me. Lord, help me to heed Your timing as to the best time to speak what You give me. Let me touch _____'s heart with my words and Your wisdom. Thank You, Lord. In Jesus' name, Amen.

22

Submission

James 4:7 "Therefore submit to God. Resist the devil and he will flee from you."

Submission is a foreign concept to American culture, I think. For the most part, we are an individualistic society that is concerned with our personal rights and privileges. To subject oneself to others or yield to their authority is often difficult for us at any age. Given that college-age young people are just discovering their freedom, asking them to submit is akin to restraining them once again. In actuality, to submit is not to be restrained. It requires an exertion of freedom. It is an active choice. Once young people realize that they can willingly make the decision to submit, it does not seem quite so bad.

Submission to God is a beautiful position for your child. It is in this position that your son or daughter can safely resist the devil and he will flee; hallelujah! In this position of humility, your child will receive the grace that God promises to the humble, and He exalts those who are humble before Him (1 Pet 5:6, 7). It is so exciting to think of God lifting up our children and placing them right where they should be. Often that place is right in the middle of their hearts' desires!

In addition, being in full submission to God enables them to submit to those in authority over them. Despite the "I'm free" thoughts your child may be having in regard to being in college and away from home, he or she will still need to answer to people in higher authority. If your son or daughter can do this with genuine humility and respect, college life and communication will be more pleasant than it would be without it. Let's pray that your young person chooses submission.

Father, may _____ realize the importance of submission; first to You, and then to those in authority. I pray that _____'s desire will be to honor You by humbly bowing heart and knee to You in total submission. Lord, let this not be a strange or foreign concept to _____. Instead, please reveal to _____ the freedom that comes with submitting to Your will. What an incredibly safe place for my child to be, God, and that is in the center of Your will! I pray, Lord, that _____ will be an example of proper submission to the college professors, and to all those who have authority over _____. Thank You, my King, for Your precious Word and promises. Thank You for Your work in _____'s life. In Jesus' name, Amen.

23

Trust

Proverbs 3:5 "Trust in the Lord with all your heart, and lean not on your own understanding."

Trust implies reliance. How many of us have trusted in ourselves and our false presumptions that we had everything in our lives figured out? My supposed understanding has failed me more times than I'd like to count. Even after all these years of knowing and trusting God, I find myself still trying to figure things out on my own more often than I care to admit. If we, the more mature and experienced adults, tend to rely on our own limited understanding, we can certainly imagine that our young adults are doing the same. This is not necessarily due to our influence (in this case), but because they are striving to be adults who have it all together. I think we all enjoy giving the appearance that we know exactly what is going on in our lives. I believe it causes us to feel more confident and secure if we have the answers, or, at least, think we have them.

Trust also implies dependence. I believe that we should want our children to depend on what they know to be true, and in what they have learned. Primarily, I believe that we want them to trust and depend in God and what they know about Him. There will be many opportunities in college for your child to rely on self, others, and things. That will be okay to a point, as long as God is at the foundation of that reliance and your child's focus remains on the fact that God is truly the only One who is totally dependable and trustworthy. God can be taken at His Word every time. Let's pray that your child remembers God has his or her best interests at heart and can be trusted to provide direction and wisdom in every situation.

God, I pray that _____ will always trust in You and what _____ knows to be true of You. Place within _____ Your instincts, Your voice, and give _____ the trust to rely on You. Let _____ not trust in self, others, or things to the detriment of Your ways in _____ life. Let _____ always stand on what _____ knows to be right and true. Take away any deception the enemy would use in an attempt to sway _____ from the belief that You are always trustworthy. The enemy is a liar and the father of lies. Protect and fill _____'s heart with the assurance and confidence that _____ can trust You for always. Thank You, Lord. Amen.

24

Joy

Psalm 5:11 "But let all those rejoice who put their trust in You; let them ever shout for joy, because You defend them; let those also who love Your name be joyful in You."

As Jonathan grew, the joy of the Lord that he expressed was such an encouragement to me. He radiated trust and confidence in the Lord. His demeanor said, "Everything is going to be okay. It's not that bad." He was not at all easily shaken by circumstances. His friends at college found this "attitude" to be annoying during Jon's first year there. They just did not understand why he did not get upset as they did. To him, it seemed as if the smallest irritation (molehill) could be made into a mountain by his friends. To them, it seemed as if Jon had no molehills, much less mountains. I remember an occasion, when he was a young child, in which he said, "Mom, it's just water, it will dry." That time it really was water, but I was anxious about the situation. That, however, became a principle which I began to apply to other potentially anxiety-ridden occurrences. God used that thinking to grow my faith and trust in Him.

As the above verse reveals, joy comes from relationship with God. It comes from loving and trusting Him, and from knowing that He is the protector. Just typing these words causes great delight to well up within my heart! Oh, that your college child would know and walk in this incredible joy! College is going to be a very busy place for your son or daughter if he or she is dedicated to education (and perhaps some fun). This busyness could rob your child of joy. Busyness has a way of squeezing out God if we are not careful, and that leads to a lack of relationship with Him. As Jon got busier and busier with each successive year, we saw his joy wane as his active relationship with God suffered. Let us pray that your child will not have that same experience.

Oh Lord, what great joy is experienced in relationship with You! I pray that _____ will know You, trust You, love You, and depend on You. I pray that _____'s heart will overflow with the joy of the Lord as _____ walks in intimate relationship with You. Let _____ not get so caught up in the busyness of school and life that _____ drifts away from a close walk with You. If _____ is in that place now, Lord, please restore to _____ the joy of Your salvation. Strengthen and encourage _____ heart to stay close to You. May the joy of the Lord be so expressed in _____'s life, that others come to know You as a result. Thank You, sweet Jesus. Amen.

25

Faith

Mark 11:22 "So Jesus answered and said to them, 'Have faith in God.'"

It is so comforting to me that Jesus taught on faith. When He spoke the above words, He was speaking to my heart as much as to the disciples who were right there in front of Him. To me, because it was Jesus speaking, it comes with an extra assurance that faith is indeed powerful and life-transforming. Think of the numerous verses in which Jesus said something like, "Your faith has made you well." The faith of the people to whom He spoke carried great power that allowed them to experience God at work in their lives. Think about when He told the young woman, "Your faith has saved you" (Luke 7:50). Talk about life-transforming! I think we can safely assume that this young woman walked a different walk after that encounter. Oh, the glory of the Lord! I have to add this comment: I am absolutely astounded that God gives us the very faith that it takes to even believe in Him. We just have to say yes to it.

It is my belief that faith creates a foundation upon which your child can walk confidently and assuredly in the many places/encounters/situations that college will provide. Faith in God will bring the knowledge and comfort that he or she is not ever alone. It will bring the belief that he or she can accomplish the things that God has set out in front, and that He will provide the strength needed to remain on the right path. Faith will increase the ability for your child to learn, retain, articulate, and project, because your young person will know that God is there directing and strengthening. Faith provides a secure belief that the person (or thing) in which faith has been placed, in this case God, is fully trust-worthy. To *trust* is to rely on, whereas to have *faith* is to believe. Let's pray together that your child will have faith in the One who alone is truly reliable.

Dear Lord, I pray that _____ will have great faith that allows _____ to believe in You with _____ whole heart. Faith in You brings security and confidence that You are active and involved in our lives. Increase _____'s faith to believe that You will guide and direct in every area of _____ life. May _____ walk securely in the awareness that You are completely believable and trustworthy. Give _____ faith to continue on the path that You have set before _____. May faith rise within _____'s heart and empower _____ to stay the course when opportunities come to be led astray. Lord, allow _____ to experience the life-changing power that faith in You provides. Thank You, Lord. In Jesus' powerful name, Amen.

26

Faithfulness

Galatians 5:22, 23 "But the fruit of the Spirit is love, joy, peace, longsuffering, kindness, goodness, faithfulness, gentleness, self-control. Against such there is no law."

The first thought that comes to mind when I think of this topic is the faithfulness of the Lord. I can sing along with the Psalmist as he declares, "I will sing of the mercies of the LORD forever; With my mouth will I make known Your faithfulness to all generations" (89:1). I used to think that I could not learn much from the Old Testament, other than some history. I looked to the New Testament when seeking to know God's heart and His direction. How mistaken I was to have read through the Old Testament in a perfunctory manner. Oh, I did always love the personal stories, such as those about Moses and Joseph, but I found myself almost separating the God of Israel from the God of love that I had discovered in the New Testament. Wow, was I so wrong! I read the Old Testament now and truly see God's heart and love evidenced by His incredible faithfulness to His people.

I am constantly amazed and grateful for God's kindness and faithfulness to me and my family. Oh, dear parent, I hope you recognize the Lord's faithfulness in your life and the life of your child. My prayer is that your child is so aware of God's faithfulness that he or she chooses to walk in faithfulness, first to Him and then to His plan. I believe this college "season" in your young person's life is preparation for what is to come. May he or she be faithful in this time period and to this task, so that a firm groundwork of faithfulness is built. There is a great need for faithfulness and loyalty in our society. I think those who exhibit these traits will stand out among others when interviewing for jobs, seeking to advance in career, building lasting relationships, and ministering in the Lord's name. These are people who can be trusted in and depended upon. We will pray that your son or daughter exhibits faithfulness in everything to which he or she sets mind and hand.

Dear Lord, thank You for Your great faithfulness. I am overwhelmed. I pray, Lord, that _____ will know and walk in Your faithfulness. Let _____ life be characterized by faithfulness to You and all to which You call _____. While _____ is in college, lay the foundation of faithfulness in _____ life. I pray that _____ will be faithful in all _____ relationships and that You will protect those relationships. Father, I do pray that the fruit of the Spirit would so fill and overflow from _____'s heart and life that others will come to know You because they have known _____. In Jesus' name, Amen.

27

Thrive

Psalm 46:10 "Be still, and know that I am God…"

How many people do you know who just seem to be surviving from day to day? They are doing only what they need to in order to make it to the next day. Then they get up and do it all over again. I realize that much of life is routine, and I personally think that is a good thing. I am not talking about structure and order. I am talking about thoughts and attitudes. Surviving is little more than merely existing. In my mind, it connotes striving with each day, occasion, or situation as it comes. I think of it as doing only what it takes to get by, barely making it, and hanging on for dear life. There is a mentality there that bespeaks of nothing better and nothing more. It is a mentality that settles for less than the best. In reality, it is a mentality that does not even recognize that better truly does exist. It is an awful mindset that can become ingrained in one's very being.

Certainly this is not what we want for our young people. The verse above speaks to the hope and confidence of there really being more. There is so much more than meager circumstances. We do not have to constantly strive to just get by and "accept our lot" in life. As you grab hold of this truth and speak it into as well as pray it for your child's life, what incredible joy this could bring to your college child. "Stop the striving, child. Be still! Know the God who knows your circumstances and wants so much more for you. Know the God who will grow and flourish you." Your child does not have to merely survive young adulthood and college while waiting for something else. He or she can thrive throughout these amazing years. Let's pray just that way!

Dear Lord, how mighty and awesome You are! To know You is to trust, love, and bless You. Thank You that we can really know You. Father, I pray that _____ will cease striving in all areas. Young people tend to strive for popularity, acceptance, and control. I pray against these kinds of struggles in my child's life. Lord, I speak against the schemes of the enemy to engage and trap _____ in the awful mindset of this is all there is. You are God, and You cause Your people to thrive, to grow vigorously, and to flourish. Lord, this is what I pray for _____. May _____ grow in the things of You and all that You have for _____. May _____ never settle for less than what You have as _____ best. I pray that _____ will truly be still and know who You are in _____ life, and that just having this knowledge will cause his heart and mind to thrive. Thank You, my loving God. Amen.

28

Health

3 John 1:2 "Beloved, I pray that you may prosper in all things and be in health, just as your soul prospers."

Other than a few ear infections in infancy and an occasional strep throat since then, Jonathan has always been a healthy person. In fact, he can tell you exactly how many times he has thrown up since he was a toddler because they have been so few in number (I know, ugh). I am so thankful for this incredible and blessed gift from the Lord. I know He led us to do many things that aided this blessing. I gave Jonathan vitamins nearly everyday. He did not often eat candy and pastries as a child. He has always loved salads and veggies, which we served regularly. We had routine bedtimes which allowed for adequate time to sleep in order to be restored and refreshed. He found joy and strength in the Lord. Doing things that would lead to his good health was definitely a priority of mine.

This remained a focus during his college years. Unfortunately, he did not stay as healthy. Many issues played a factor in his acquiring several severe colds, viruses, etc. He certainly slept less and went out more. He was part of a busy, hectic program which kept him going at a frenetic pace. He did not always have food, much less healthy food, at his fingertips. When asked if he was taking his vitamins, often his reply was, "When I think about it." In addition to not filling himself with the things that would lead to good health, he was inundated with stress which hinders the health of both mind and body. His soul was no longer prospering because He was spending little time with the Lord and in God's Word. I believe that God can help us achieve balancing acts in our busy lives while allowing us to maintain healthiness in body and soul. Let's pray this for your child.

Lord, just as John prayed, I do pray that _____ will prosper in all things. Give _____ wisdom to make good decisions that will strengthen _____ spirit, soul, and body. Lord, may You be first in _____'s life. May _____ prosper in mind, will, emotions, spirit, and health as _____ looks to You to be _____ strength, guide, and joy. Help _____ to balance the many demands that college brings. Father, I pray that _____ will be kept from illness and poor health. Teach _____ to heed Your prompting regarding eating, resting, and making good decisions. May _____ always be strong and healthy. Thank You, Jesus. Amen.

29

Focus

Colossians 3:2 "Set your mind on things above, not on things on the earth."

There is so much in our daily lives to distract us from our focus. Work distracts us from play; play distracts us from work; doubt creates fear, which then distracts us from pressing ahead. On and on it goes. Some days I feel as if I am constantly pulling my attention back to the task or thought at hand. Even in prayer. I discover the importance of focus more and more each day. The object of my focus is the key to how I will handle the current circumstance. If I focus on the tumult, as Peter did on the winds and the waves (Matthew 14:30), I struggle and find it difficult to see my way out. When I change my focus to finding solutions or resolutions, I discover that something can be done to alter the situation. Above all, when I focus on Christ as my wisdom and guide, it is then that I find hope and strength in the midst of any circumstance. This is the primary focus I desire for my child and yours.

Jon discovered that college is a place where great focus is needed and distracting opportunities abound! There were always so many people and things that called (yelled, sometimes) for his attention. We can pretty much assume that your college child will discover the same. Those voices may beckon your child to good things, better things, or unimportant and frivolous things. Whatever the call and whatever the motivation behind it, your child will need to maintain sharp focus so that he or she is not deterred from the best things. He or she does not have to be dragged down or away from focus on God, classes, homework, studying, and goals. In my life, it takes the power and strength of God to keep me consistently on the right path with my focus. Even while writing this book, I have found that sheer determination and conviction have not been enough to keep bringing me back to it. It has taken crying out to God often to motivate me and help me to focus. Let us cry out for your child to focus on Him, so that He can empower him or her to focus on the important.

Oh Lord, I want my child to set _____ mind on things above, starting with You. May _____ so love and desire You that _____ walks closely with You and trusts You to guide _____. Lord, help _____ to maintain focus on the important goals and things of life. Please keep _____ from being distracted by the lure of the world and all that it offers. Lord, I pray that You will reveal deception to _____ when something posing as good is not the best. Help _____ to discern what voices to heed and what paths to take. May _____ focus on doing well in college so that _____ learns all that You have for _____ there. Strengthen _____ resolve to maintain the direction and focus that You provide. Thank You, Jesus. Amen.

30

Compassion

1 Peter 3:8 "Finally, all of you be of one mind, having compassion for one another; love as brothers, be tenderhearted, be courteous."

Jonathan's compassion has cost us many times, in good ways. We began support of our first World Vision child because his heart went out to the needy children in the television commercials. Supporting Klove radio became a priority because he wanted others to hear about the love of Jesus so that they might be saved. Now that he earns an income, he donates to St. Jude because he was moved with compassion when he visited the hospital. I believe these things are certainly of God's heart. If you read through the New Testament, you will find many examples of Jesus acting with compassion. His heart genuinely cared for people and about their distresses. God's compassion is extolled throughout the Old Testament. We could all probably share many stories of how we have experienced the compassion and comfort of our loving God.

There are three areas on which I would like to focus regarding prayer for your college child to have compassion. One: the Lord is full of compassion and we are made in His

Surround Your College Child with Prayer

image. Unfortunately, we image-bearers are not always accurately displaying the image that God would have us display. Two: sometimes compassion can become skewed if one is not wise, and then there is the danger of being taken advantage of and mistreated. Three: some who are compassionate tend to "take on" the distress of others and become burdened to a point of emotional unhealthiness. Christ gave us examples of reaching out and touching the hurting, and we know He wants us to be compassionate. We also know He wants us to use wisdom. It is my desire that my child and yours have compassionate hearts, making a difference in the lives of those around them and in the world as God leads. I pray that they will exercise wisdom when choosing what to do and for whom. I do not want them to be gullible, and therefore used and abused for their efforts. I desire that they be emotionally healthy, so that when they do help others they will not begin to carry their distress. This, too, will enable them to be more effective when helping others. Let's seek the Lord for the compassion of your child.

Lord, thank You for giving us examples of Your compassion and calling us to be compassionate people. I pray that _____ will have genuine compassion and that it will move _____ to help others. Lord, give _____ sound wisdom as ___ ___ seeks to alleviate distress and help _____ to be effective in touching those around _____. I pray that others will not attempt to use and abuse _____ kindness and caring. Please give _____ emotional healthiness and protect that as _____ cares for others. When _____ needs compassion, I pray that there will be others to show it to _____. Enrich _____'s life, I pray, as _____ blesses others. Thank You, Lord. Amen.

74

31

Leadership

1 Timothy 4:12 "Let no one despise your youth, but be an example to the believers in word, in conduct, in love, in spirit, in faith, in purity."

The two words that quickly come to my mind when I think of leadership are *example* and *servant*. I have witnessed many examples of quality leadership, and I have seen some examples of poor leadership as well. There are several characteristics that I have found to be common among good leaders. Good leaders care about the people they lead. The people are more important than the job or project. They care not only about the quality of work put forth by these individuals, but also about the quality of their own work. Good leaders are often motivated to become better leaders because of the people they serve. The best leaders are those who serve because they want to set an example, and because they want their people to learn, grow, and even exceed the leader's abilities. They want to inspire their people to aspire to greater things. Many people would agree that Jesus exampled servant-leadership. He operated in authority, but was not self-seeking or prideful. There is absolutely no doubt or argument that He was, indeed, a servant.

In contrast, poor leaders are often restrictive because they want to make sure they are seen as the ones making things happen (forget serving others). They want everyone under their authority to do well, but only well enough to make them (the leaders) look good. Sharing the credit for a job well done is not found among this bunch of leaders. Their motivation to become better leaders is not for the people under them, it is for the "higher-ups." I guess it comes down to this: good leaders are others-focused, and poor leaders are self-focused. Naturally we want our children to not only be good leaders and have those wonderful characteristics mentioned in the first paragraph, we also want them to be under the authority of good leaders. There will be opportunities for both in college. Let's pray that your child chooses to follow wise leaders, and that he or she takes advantage of positive leadership experiences.

Dear Lord, I pray that _____ will have good, strong leaders who will genuinely care about _____ while in college. May they be positive role models for _____ so that _____ learns about good leadership firsthand. Please reveal any deception that could cause _____ to follow after those who are self-seeking. Give _____ opportunities to be a leader and let _____ learn to lead in a way that pleases and honors You. May these experiences further develop _____ into the person You have destined _____ to be. Thank You for the incredible testimony of Jesus as He came to serve. In His precious name, Amen.

32

Love

Song of Solomon 3:5 "...Do not stir up nor awaken love until it pleases."

Ipray that your college child will love the Lord with all of his or her heart, soul, mind, and strength (Mark 12:30). Next, I pray that all else will flow from that place to his or her other relationships. It is precisely on these horizontal relationships that I want to focus. College sometimes becomes a place of practicing for some. It is a time of growing up and experimenting with adult life issues. In the midst of this learning, young people often form relationships in the name of love that are harmful. Fragile emotions become damaged and a sense of neediness often occurs. God did create us with a need to love and be loved; first in relationship to Him, and then in relationship to others. It is no surprise, then, that Satan takes that natural desire and deceives people into thinking they must fill that need in their way and their time. He weaves deception to create neediness and a false sense of control. We are all susceptible; and young people seem especially to be swayed when they encounter situations in which it seems that anything is allowed and anything goes. College sometimes gives this impression.

Through conversations with my son and others, I have heard about many young people's relationships that are a hindrance to their lives, but yet they hang on through constant pain and upset. It is as if they think life could not exist without that other person and the "love" they feel. Some live together and then walk away with nothing of value, only fragmented hearts. I do not believe it is God's heart that our children have intimate relationship after intimate relationship. God is truth, and He wants our children to discern between truth and deception. I want Jonathan to recognize true love and to wait for the young woman that God knows is just right for him, and he just right for her. I do not want him caught up in the world's definition of love, of what makes him happy with no concern for others. Love is so much more than a feeling, so much more than pleasure. It is also a choice and a commitment. This is an important time to pray that love is not awakened in your child before its' proper time.

Father, I thank You that You love _____ more than I ever could. I thank You that You have given _____ the capacity to give and receive love. May _____ receive Your love in its' fullness and love You with _____ whole being. Lord, I pray that You will guard _____'s heart and mind as _____ forms relationships with others. Keep _____ from forming harmful relationships, and Lord protect _____ from those who would desire to lead _____ astray into ungodliness in the name of love. I pray that _____ waits for Your timing and Your mate before giving _____ heart to another. May _____ so clearly desire Your life-long helpmate that _____ recognizes Your design and direction in this area of life. Once _____ has found this true love, please surround and protect them and their relationship for life. Thank You, Jesus. Amen.

33

Beyond College

Jeremiah 29:11 "For I know the thoughts that I think toward you, says the LORD, thoughts of peace and not of evil, to give you a future and a hope."

College graduation, wow! Time flies, doesn't it?! What an exciting time this will be for your child. Surely he or she will be glad to leave the homework behind and have a break. There will be pride and a great sense of accomplishment. Even so, it may also be a time of sadness, uncertainty, and fear. Your child will be leaving a place that has become familiar to once again enter into a future of unfamiliarity. He or she has spent a few years seeing some of the same faces from day to day. Friendships have been built and it will be hard to leave these people behind. They will go from being right around the corner from one another to possibly being around the world from one another. Sure, they can text, Facebook, and call one another, but it just won't be the same. This is definitely a time in which emotions seem to be riding a roller coaster.

Now comes "real life." Your child is faced with becoming an adult and taking on all the responsibilities that come with this role. That sounds a little scary, even to me. Resumes and applications will seem to fly out as your son or daughter now puts education to the test. Your son may question whether or not he really learned all that he needed to get a good job. Your daughter is likely questioning if she did indeed do well enough in her schoolwork to prove that she is capable. The ultimate question, I think, has to do with the fact that he or she probably went to college in order to pursue a career, not just a job. "Was this education enough to launch me onto my career path?" So many questions, so many uncertainties. God does have a plan for your child. He created him or her with purpose. That does not mean, of course, that fulfilling God's purpose is going to be easy. My boss recently pointed out that when the Lord spoke the above message (verse) to Jeremiah, He was speaking it to His people who were in captivity. That certainly could not have been an easy time, but God assured them that He held their future. Just as He holds the future of your college child. Let's pray for what He has.

Dear Lord, I thank You for Your faithfulness to my child throughout these years of college. Thank You for enabling _____ to finish well. Please protect _____'s heart and mind as this transition takes place and as _____ leaves people behind. Lord, only You know exactly what thoughts and questions are swirling about in _____'s mind. Give _____ peace and increase _____ faith, I pray. Let _____ not be anxious for anything but trust You in all things regarding the future. Place Your calling upon _____'s life and lead _____ right to that place. I know that where You call, You equip; and that is a place of great joy and fulfillment. Thank You, God. I am so grateful. Amen.

CPSIA information can be obtained at www.ICGtesting.com
Printed in the USA
LVOW041337110412

277174LV00001B/23/P